I0558341

HOW TO SURVIVE
THE DEATH OF A
LOVED
ONE

HOW TO SURVIVE
THE DEATH OF A
LOVED ONE

John Chris Brown

ARPress
ILLUMINATING IDEAS
EMPOWERING VOICES

Copyright © 2022 by John Chris Brown

All rights reserved. No part of this publication may be reproduced, distributed, or transmitted in any form or by any means, including, photocopying,recording, or other electronic or mechanical methods, without the prior written permission of the copyright owner and the publisher, except in the case of brief quotations embodied in critical reviews and certain other noncommercial uses permitted by copyright law. For permission requests, write to the publisher, addressed "Attention: Permissions Coordinator," at the address below.

ARPress
45 Dan Road Suite 5
Canton MA 02021

Hotline: 1(888) 821-0229
Fax: 1(508) 545-7580

Ordering Information:
Quantity sales. Special discounts are available on quantity purchases by corporations, associations, and others. For details, contact the publisher at the address above.

Printed in the United States of America.
ISBN-13:   Paperback   979-8-89330-868-6
             eBook   979-8-89330-869-3

Library of Congress Control Number: 2024901847

Contents

Dedication

This book is dedicated to the memory of every loved one we have lost. It's dedicated to those of us who have been left here in the earthly realm to cherish precious memories and who look forward to the day we will be reunited in the presence of God. To my wives, Bertha Mae Brown, Jimmy L. Brown, Dede R. Brown, my mother Wilma F. Brown, my in-laws Bishop Horace Stacey II and First Lady Billie J. Stacey, my uncle Clevester Gaither, thank you all for the love, the beautiful memories, life lessons, and spiritual guidance you left me with. I'd like to thank my children Kristie M. Taylor, Marquito D. Craig, Christopher C. Brown, and Deziree R. Biggins and my 7 grandchildren for their never-ending love and support. You all are my most prized blessings, and I will forever pray God's divine destiny and favor over your lives. To my readers, God loves you and so do I. I pray that peace and comfort find you and that you rest in the bosom of the almighty savior Jesus Christ. Peace and blessings. Bishop John C. Brown

HOW TO SURVIVE THE DEATH OF A LOVED ONE

By: JOHN BROWN

Christian scripture and touching memoir combine in this honest, enheartening guide for those who are mourning or facing the prospect of losing a family member or close friend. Author Brown began to realize the challenges of such trauma and tragedy with the loss of his first wife to cancer when both were young and caring for their first child. As he recalls, he grieved deeply while painfully perceiving the needs of his toddler child who lacked her mother's presence. The concern of a caring group of friends and family helped him to cope. He married again, but his second wife also died of cancer, leaving Brown once more with children to care for while nurturing his own sense of emptiness. Then, after serving with him in his Christian leadership, a third wife developed cancer, passing after twenty-two years, making him a widower once more. These losses and others caused the author to contemplate the complexities of grief and develop a wider understanding of God's plan for all.

Brown is the pastor of a community church who frequently visits and prays with the sick and afflicted. Through his personal tragedies and strong Christian faith, he has the will and comprehension to advise others and does so here with a sincere purpose. Throughout this compassionate look at the grieving process, Brown asserts that faith in God will help His followers hold to a path to peace after the passing away of a close companion. His short but powerful treatise is frank regarding his feelings and inspirational as he provides copious relevant references from the Holy Bible to support his conviction that despite the earthly sorrows people must go through, and as heartrending as such events may be, there is hope for renewed contentment here and a blissful, eternal reward.

-US REVIEW OF BOOKS

Chapter 1

How to Survive the Death of a Loved One

"Grief" is defined as "intense sorrow: great sadness, especially as a result of a death." Intro: Whenever we lose someone we love, we need to know and understand the purpose of what has happened. Even though many of us find the subject of death unpleasant, it is a fact of life that we all must face. The Bible tells us it is once appointed for man to die; and after that, the judgment (Heb. 9:27). The grief experience after the death of a loved one can be very painful. It touches all ages, all races, all cultures, and all socioeconomic groups. No matter how many times we experience it, there is an accompanying feeling of sorrow that is common to the human experience. One reason I decided to tell my story is because this is a subject people tend to avoid and never understand. You need to know that there is a healing process whenever you deal with the reality of the loss of a loved one. We tend to avoid talking about something that makes us uncomfortable, but it is always in the back of our minds. We don't like to entertain the thought that it will happen to us. I am a living testimony that the Lord will give you the strength that you need to survive the pain you feel after a loss. I have had to endure the pain of becoming a widower three times in my life. Many people find it strange that one would have to endure such grief. I'm a believer, as were all my wives, and we should understand that believers are not exempt from loss. In addition to this (in close proximity) was the death of my biological mother, my mother-in-law, and my uncle. All of this transpired within a three-year time span. Let me be transparent and share with you some of my personal experiences I've had to encounter. Right after high school, I met a young Christian lady by the name of Bertha. We both were very young in age. Her beauty caught my eyes, but it was that inward beauty that she had for her God that got my attention. She invited me to come to church with her on a Saturday night. This service was awesome, and I had never experienced a real move of God like I did that night. I felt the convicting power of the Holy Spirit. I felt the Holy Spirit immediately began to deal with my heart. It was as though I had been tagged by God and was irresistibly drawn to Him. Bertha was a true worshiper of God and had already been born again, but at this time in my life, I was trying to learn more about God. I did not know the Lord on a personal level like she did at that time. I did not know at the time that God was using her to help me walk in my God given destiny.In 1982, after a couple of visits to her church, I surrendered my life to God. Pastor Horace Stacey II was the presiding overseer of the church at that time. We became very close. He was my mentor, my best friend, and my spiritual father; and the love I had for him was great. I had found the place where I fit. Bertha and I fell in love and were married about one year later. Not long after, we had our first-born daughter, Kristie. We were very much in love and very happy. Life was good. Never could we have imagined that after my wife gave birth to Kristie, that disease was developing in her body and would soon take her life. She became very sick over time, and we found out that cancer had taken over her body, and she eventually died at a very early age. Two years and eight months after saying our vows, I became a young widower with the task of raising our only daughter. I felt like a dead man walking among the living after Bertha died. This was a very painful experience. I am so thankful that I was a part of a ministry that provided support. A good support system is indispensable in times like this.We need godly believers to help us find a way through personal tragedy. I found the strength I needed through and with the help of my church family. It is important that we surround ourselves with strong people. The Lord placed many other women in my daughter's life to help give her the love that she needed. I can remember her at age one and a half missing her mother's love and wondering where she was.I saw my daughter go through the grieving process as a toddler crying to see her mother's face and be in her presence. As she got older, she wondered about her mother's personality and favorite things. She wondered how it would have felt to be held in her mother's arms and comforted by her or to have her mother present for milestones, or special events in her life. She missed the opportunity to be able to confide in her mother about normal everyday things and challenges that young women face. Many times, she asked me about her mother. I filled in as much information as I could, but it was not like having her mother present with her or having her own account and memories of her mother. I'm sure she wondered how things might have been different if her mother had lived. The Lord blessed her with aunts and grandmothers to try and help fill the void her mother left, but there is nothing like a mother's love. I have watched this baby grow up to be a great woman of God that I am very proud of. She has learned to hold on to the promises of God even in her pain. I thank God that I am a man of faith who was able to raise and train my children in the ways of the Lord. The Lord has been faithful in his promises. In 1987, two years after the death of my first wife, I remarried. My second wife, Jimmie, gave birth to two children, Marquito and Christopher. I was very happy and blessed to have her as my wife. Three and a half years into the marriage, she also began to experience some type of sickness. She was diagnosed with breast cancer. She endured this sickness for two years after the diagnosis, which eventually lead to her death as well. We were married five years and six months. And here I was again in the same situation of dealing with the death of another spouse. This was one of the times in life that I felt like giving up on God. You cannot imagine the questions that ran through my mind and the feeling of being abandoned by God. I was a single father with three children to raise. Marquito and Christopher also went through the same struggles as my oldest daughter, Kristie, even though they were a few years older than Kristie when their mother passed. Marquito was four years and six months old, and Christopher was two years and six months old. Marquito and Christopher went through the grieving process after their mother, Jimmie, passed as well. Thank God that they also had others in their lives to help fill the void of the loss of their mother. I am very proud of Marquito and Christopher; they have both grown to be successful and responsible young adults. The Lord has been faithful and helped us as a family to survive. I knew that the Lord was my only hope. I knew God still had a plan for my life, and I knew that the Lord would never leave me nor forsake me. The Lord again restored and healed my broken state. The enemy tried his best to steal my joy. In life, you will have to endure many things. It may feel as though you are going around the same mountain over and over, but the scripture says, "If you suffer with him you will reign with him" (2 Tim. 2:12). As the saying goes, "He never promised us a rose garden, but he did promise to be with us." I knew that my life was not over, and I knew that God had something else in store for me. I continued to seek God for the direction of my life. I threw myself into the ministry and was given additional responsibility to serve as the assistant pastor. The pressures of single fatherhood, my responsibility to the ministry, and still trying to heal from my losses encouraged me to seek God like never before. At this point in my life, I was a single father raising three children; but with the help of God and my church family, I was able to keep my head above water. Sometimes, that's all we can do, to just keep swimming. Being a young man, I did have a desire to marry again. I learned how to pray and put God first in my life. I knew that whatever I needed, He would provide for me. I also knew that being a man of God in a position of leadership, I could not be unequally yoked with an unbeliever. There was a Godly, talented, attractive, young lady that I knew and had worshiped with over the years. Neither of us had any idea that God was preparing her to be my wife. We eventually started communicating with one another and fell in love. We married in 1994, and Dede became my third wife. She was a powerful woman of God as well as a great mother to my children. She also served alongside me as the First Lady of the church that I now pastor. We raised four children together, Kristie, Marquito, Christopher, and Deziree. She was diagnosed with stage four colon cancer; and after twenty-two years and two months of a wonderful marriage, the Lord called her home to glory August 2015. I can say that I was favored and blessed to have lived and enjoyed life together with this great woman. Again, for the third time in my life, I am completely devastated by the loss of another spouse. All of my children have dealt with the loss of their mothers. I am blessed to have four children. My youngest, Deziree, was twenty-four years old when her mother, DeDe, passed away. Even though she is an adult, it was very painful and difficult for her to watch her mother suffer with cancer. When her mother went home to be with the Lord, Deziree also went through the grieving process even though she was older than the others when her mother died. Deziree is blossoming and becoming a wonderful young lady. I know she misses her mother a lot because I do having been married to her for twenty-two years and two months. With God's help, I've continued to be a good father, pastor, mentor, and grandfather. God has been faithful, and my family still standing. There are additional things that I will share with you about my struggles, and I pray that as you read each chapter of this book that it will bless you immensely. Keep in mind that everyone must die. Early in life, we acquire distorted views about death, we focus on the acquisition of things, but we must learn that not only do good things come into our lives but we will also experience loss. We are people of God who are created after His own image and likeness, and we were created to live forever. Sin brought death upon the earth, and now we suffer the consequence, which is death. Adam was told by God that in the day that he ate from the tree of the knowledge of good and evil, he will surely die (Gen. 2:17). A biblical perspective and faith in God will help us to understand death. Scriptural teaching can bring clarification and answer many questions that we might have concerning the subject of death. It is possible to experience the peace of God that surpasses all understanding even during loss. The more you know, the better understanding and peace of mind you will have. Surviving the loss of a loved one is possible with adequate biblical information. Here are some things that I would like for you to consider. What can we learn in the Bible that can shed some light on the reason why people die? What does the Scripture say about death? If we would only take a little time and research the scriptures, we can learn why death occurs. We do not have to remain in the dark about death. Many people have distorted views about death, and they have questions about where one will spend eternity when they die. My belief is based on the word of God. I know of no other source that will give you better insight on the subject about death. In the book of Genesis, the Bible gives us the story of Adam and Eve. As I've stated before, man was created to live forever and was placed in the garden to have perfect fellowship with God. The Bible lets us know that Adam was made from the dust of the ground, and God breathed into him the breath of life and Adam became a living being. If Adam obeyed the instructions that were given to him by God, he would continue to live. We know the outcome. Adam sinned and as a result of his sin, death was passed to mankind. But God, in His infinite wisdom, provided a way for man to be reconciled to Him and not have to die eternally. This was brought about by the descending of His son, Jesus Christ, who died in our place. The Lord set up boundaries in the Garden of Eden to save Adam's life, as long as he obeyed all the instructions that the Lord commanded him to do he would continue to live. God was thinking about Adam's best interest. God also wants you to live and enjoy your life. God put Adam in the Garden of Eden to take care of it and more importantly to have fellowship with Him. And the Lord God instructed and commanded the man, "You are free to eat from any tree in the garden; but you must not eat from the tree of the knowledge of good and evil, for when you eat of it you will surely die" (Gen. 2:16–17). How much better would our life be if we listened and obeyed God's instructions? We can see that as a result of Adam's sin death became a consequence. "The wages of sin is death, but the gift of God is eternal life" (Rom. 6:23). "For since death came through a man, the resurrection of the dead comes also through a man. For as in Adam all die, so in Christ all will be made alive" (1 Cor. 15:21–22). Let us also understand that death is a blessed release from an imperfect world for the Christian. For those who hope in Christ, we look forward to death because we know what is on the other side. It is not a mystery to us. God has made it clear, Jesus has prepared a place for us. Our hope is secure in Him because Christ paid the price for our sin. He has defeated death! One moment in God's kingdom will be worth all the pain and suffering that we go through in this life. Romans 8:18 states, "For I reckon that the sufferings of this present time are not worthy to be compared with the glory which shall be revealed in us." God had a remedy and a plan for mankind. Even though Adam died morally and spiritually, that did not mean that he would have to die eternally. It did not mean that fellowship with God would be totally terminated. Remember God foreshadowing the death of His son, slew an animal, and used the coats of skin to cover Adam and Eve. Even in the garden, God provided a substitute. You can see that you can experience the peace of God even in the midst of loss. There is peace in God when you are a believer, but for those who do not hope in Christ, the thought of death is misery. The thought of believing in nothing after a person has died is a scary thought. Jesus makes all the difference if you are going to survive this kind of pain. How can we be certain about what is to come on the other side of death? Christ's resurrection is a guarantee! It is not just a religious belief. It is a historical fact that Jesus rose from the dead. Since Jesus rose from the dead, we are guaranteed that we will also be resurrected as well. The 1 Corinthians 15:20–23 states, "But now is Christ risen from the dead, and become the first fruits of them that slept. For since by man came death, by man came also the resurrection of the dead. For as in Adam all die, even so in Christ shall all be made alive. But every man in his own order: Christ the first fruits; after they that are Christ's at his coming." Believers can be certain of their salvation because of the promises that are in the word of God.According to the Scriptures, if Christ had not rose from the dead, then our preaching about it is useless and in vain. Being a born-again Christian, we know there is great hope whenever someone dies in Christ. That doesn't mean death is not painful, and that we will not grieve or experience sadness. The Scripture lets us know that joy and bliss await a person who dies in Christ. Therefore, we do not sorrow like unbelievers. It does not mean we aren't to miss the person who has passed away. We should be prepared for grief. It is a normal reaction to loss. We are not exempt as believers from the grieving process, but the Scripture, our faith, and belief in God make it easier to go through. Pain of a broken heart is real, pain of depression is real, pain of separation is real, and pain of loneliness is real. I experienced all of these emotions when all three of my wives died. It's hard to imagine the level pain of that one feels with the losses of this magnitude. Sometimes, we are also misled to believe that grief and mourning is a sign of weakness. The Bible says otherwise.What is grief? Grief is an important, normal response to the loss of any significant object or person. It is an experience of deprivation and anxiety, which can show itself physically, emotionally, cognitively, socially, and/or spiritually. You need to understand that there are multiple stages of grief. The stages can include but are not limited to denial, anger, bargaining, depression, and acceptance. While these are understood as stages of grief, one does not necessarily have to go through all of the stages, and the stages will certainly not occur in order and intensity will vary. But whichever stage you go through, you must go through it. Don't let anyone make you feel guilty for grieving, this is normal. Everyone's grieving process is different.Life is full of transition, people are checking in and checking out of this world we live in every day. Life is full of losses. While it is common to think of loss and grief only relating to death, life is full of other kinds of losses that can cause us to grieve. The Bible also gives us answers about how to deal with loss in general. We can experience some of the same emotions as with the death of a loved one. For example, losing a job or a house, getting a divorce, or even the loss of a pet will bring feelings of sadness. Jesus has given us permission to grieve. In His Sermon on the Mount He said, "Blessed are those who mourn, for they will be comforted" (Matt. 5:4). Even Jesus grieved. "Jesus wept" (Jn. 11:35). Jesus knew that Lazarus was about to be raised from the dead, but the Lord still grieved. He also withdrew and grieved when he learned that John the Baptist had been executed (Matt. 14:12–21). So we can know that feeling grief after a loved is a natural and inescapable part of the human experience. There are some things that we must be aware of when we are dealing with the loss of a loved one. First, we need to admit that we are grieving. Secondly, we must realize that feeling frustration, sadness, and depression is normal. Lastly, we should embrace the loss and accept the reality that our loved one is no longer physically with us. However long it takes to grieve, the grieving process is normal. Life will go on. You may think that you will never be happy again. You will. The pain of the loss will subside. And you will be able to go on with life. Having a relationship with Christ makes all the difference. Give yourself time. Do not let anyone hold you to a timeline.

Learn to be patient with yourself. Moving on does not mean you have forgotten your loved one; the goal is not to allow grief to paralyze you. Counseling can also be a beneficial tool to help one work through the different stages of grief. This may help us overcome feelings of guilt from moving on without our loved one. Connecting yourself with someone who loves you and that understands you can be very helpful as well. Surrounding yourself with spiritual people who can pray for you can also be helpful. Prayer is vital in making it through any challenge, especially grief. If you find yourself in a situation where you are in a constant state of depression and feeling hopeless, by all means, seek out professional help. There is no stigma attached, contrary to belief in the church God has gifted these people to be able to assist you. It may take more than your pastor preaching a sermon to facilitate the healing that you need. And that's ok. Get as much help as you can, and don't put it off. God doesn't want you to live the rest of your life that way. Whenever we experience loss, it does help for someone to say, "I love you," and will walk with you through this. You need love and affirmation from loved ones, and you need someone to listen to you. Surround yourself with the right group of people that can pour godly wisdom into you. As Christians, we have a responsibility to be considerate of one another. The Bible teaches us to "rejoice with those who rejoice, and mourn with those who mourn" (Rom. 12:15). Personal suffering can often teach us to be compassionate and sympathetic to others who might be experiencing a loss in their life. This is another reason why we need to be a part of the church, and we are to surround ourselves with godly people. My church family has been indispensable to help me to survive the losses that I have experienced. Losing three wives has not been easy at all. I thank the Lord that he is keeping my mind intact. Without him, I would have lost my mind.

God is good. He is the center of my joy, peace, as well as my happiness. What an awesome God we serve. The fact of the matter is that everyone will one day face grief because of the loss of a loved one or some other tragedy of life. Jesus holds the answer to our survival in these times. Jesus meets our deepest needs. He does it often times through other people Death is not the finale for believers. We are only separated from our loved ones for a time while we remain in these temporal bodies. We will one day be reunited again with the Lord. It is our faith in God that gives us this assurance. I cannot stress this enough, but you must continue to lean on the family of God for support. The earthly family can lend support; but, remember, they too may be suffering from the same loss. Learn how to live one day at a time and be not anxious for tomorrow, for tomorrow will have worries enough of its own. Remember, you will get through this with God's help. A better understanding of death is that in Christ, we simply pass from life unto life. As the Apostle Paul said, "We are confident, I say, and would prefer to be away from the body and at home with the Lord" (1 Cor. 5:8). We grieve as Christians, but not as those without hope. We can all rest in the assurances and comforts offered by our loving Lord and Savior. Take heart, Jesus loves you and knows the pain you feel. Death is universal. Even in our wedding vows, we acknowledge that one day we must release the hand of the one we love, into the hand of the one we have not yet seen; thus the phrase, "until death do us part." Death and grief can have a stern silence, but listen to the still small voice of God that will speak to you during this time. Be especially open to the voice of God when significant dates such as anniversaries, birthdays, or holidays come around. If you've recently lost your spouse, experienced the death of a child, lost a friend due to a tragic accident, if you feel your dreams were buried in the ground with your loved one, or even just standing in the soft dirt near an open grave, God can and will still speak to you. And to us, He gives this confident word found in 1 Thessalonians 4:13–4 in the Living Bible, "I want you to understand this one thing as I will continue to address what happens to a Christian when he dies so that when it happens, you will not be full of sorrow, as those who have no hope. For since we believe that Jesus died and then came back to life again, we can also believe that when Jesus returns, God will bring back with Him all the Christians who have died." So learn to cherish your memories when memories are all that remain. You can't change what has happened. You must continue to press forward. It is in these trying times that one begins to realize how dependent we are upon God. If it was an outside attacker, you could fight, but how do you fight a tumor? How do you fight a failing heart? At times like this, you feel so helpless, and all you can do is pray. The sickness of a loved one that precedes their death also takes a heavy toll on the caregivers. Often, we pray for those who are sick, but we must not forget how draining it is, both physically and emotionally, for those who are taking care of the ill person. Whether it's through a prolonged illness or a tragic accident, either way, death is hard to accept. It's never easy to lose a loved one. Death removes a significant portion of our life. You have buried more than a person; you have buried some of yourself. A part of you is taken away, and your world somehow seems diminished. When someone you love dies, it has an effect on your life. God helps us if we allow him to find a new norm. Death can come as a shock, and we feel as though the earth has shifted under our feet. We can wander around for days trying to come to grips with the reality. Never let anyone tell you not to weep or to grieve. Jesus wept at Lazarus's tomb. It is all right for us to weep, but there is no need for us to despair. I will miss Bertha, I will miss Jimmie, and I will miss Dede, but I also understand that

I will see them again in heaven if I remain in God. My soul has been anchored in the Lord. You can survive the pain, the agony, the tragedy, the loneliness, the setbacks, and the depression because you know that the Lord is with you.I am a witness that God can and will sustain you if you keep your mind stayed on him. There is nothing in the earth realm that surprises God, but just know that he said that he will be with you even until the end of the earth. Yes, I say again, "Weeping may endure for a night, but joy comes in the morning" (Ps. 30:5). I don't know about you, but I say good morning to joy. Better days are coming for you.

Chapter 2

Being Absent from the Physical Body Is To Be Made Alive in Christ

The 1 Corinthians 15:17–22 says, "And if Christ has not been raised, your faith is futile; you are still in your sins. Then those also who have fallen asleep in Christ are lost. If only for this life we have hope in Christ, we are to be pitied more than all men. But Christ has indeed been raised from the dead, the first fruits of those who have fallen asleep. For since death came through a man, the resurrection of the dead comes also through a man. For as in Adam all die, so in Christ all will be made alive." I stated before that my mother passed, my mother in law passed, and my uncle was killed in a tragic accident. My mother's passing was a shock to me because she was a seemingly healthy woman. In 2013, She had driven herself to the hospital with a minor complaint, and we believed it would be fixed without any complications. For reasons unknown to us, she was scheduled for a procedure that would not normally be performed on a woman her age. We trusted the word of her physician that everything would be all right. I saw my mother on the day of her surgery, but I had no idea that this surgery would eventually lead to events causing her death. About one week after the surgery, she died. They stated that her cause of death was cardiac arrest, myocardial infarction, and septic shock. This was devastating to me because I felt that I was cheated out of a mother. It still seems unreal, but one thing I found comfort in was that she was a saved woman and had faith in God, and she was going to meet her savior and creator on the other side. This gave me great consolation. The death of a loved can be a confusing and saddened time for all of us. We have grown over time to love these individuals; and when they die, we miss their voice, their presence, interactions with them, mannerisms, and their expressions of love for us. Death can be very heartbreaking. It is at times like these that we become aware of our own mortality and are reminded that there will be a time when we will also die.But death can be a joyous occasion for the children of God. When we pass through this veil of tears, we will enter into eternity with our Savior, we know this because God tells us that believers will be resurrected to live eternally with God.What is death? The dictionary defines *death* as the end of life, the end of biological functions. Doctors define *death* in two terms—the cessation of brain activity and the cessation of vital organ activity. As you read through the Bible, it is interesting to note that God also gives two definitions of *death*.Forever separated from God's love and mercy, the unbelieving person inherits eternal death in hell. For the vast majorityof people, an occasion, such as this, is a very sad one. It is sad for them because they have no hope. To them, death only means defeat. One's biological life may end after one passes from this life. But contrary to popular belief, it is not the final end. It is sad to say, but the unbeliever will experience eternal torment. But it doesn't have to end this way. Through Christ, we can all have eternal life in a blessed place He has prepared for us.For the believer who dies in the Lord, they just merely fall asleep because Jesus Christ has defeated death for us; and when they awake, they are in heaven. For the believing child of God, death is not the end, but a glorious new beginning. This gives us great comfort. As death and the grave could not hold Jesus, so it cannot hold those who die trusting in Christ. The Bible states, "Christ became the first fruits of those who have fallen asleep" (1 Cor. 15:23). Console yourself with the thought that even though your loved one is taken away from you, know that they are in heaven enjoying the blessings and glory that is in store for all believers. On the day that Christ returns, the believer's body will be raised from the dead and reunited with his soul in heaven. So, my friends be faithful unto death for God has promised us a crown of life.

Chapter 3

Understanding the Preciousness of Death in General

The passing of my uncle was devastating to me because it occurred on the heels of my mother's passing. My uncle was very dear to me. He was a wise man of God who often gave me advice, and who also shared my love of the Gospel. This was particularly devastating because he had just recently visited my home as a guest and he seemed to have been doing well. He was still preaching the gospel at ninety-one years old. You can imagine the sadness that I felt to learn that my uncle had been tragically killed by a hit and run driver as he crossed the street. Tragedy and unexpected death of a family member or friend is also something we may have to deal with.

Saved and unsaved alike. Again, I had to turn to the word of God for solace and to also bring me peace. I want to give you some words of comfort to help you understand the preciousness of death. "Precious in the sight of the Lord is the death of his saints" (Ps. 116:15). Why would death be precious to God? Wasn't it the entrance of sin into the world that brought forth the curse of death? Certainly. God abhors sin, and I would be willing to say that individuals in their right minds abhor the thought of dying. So, why would the death of His very children be precious to God? I think the Bible gives us some wonderful reasons. After the death of a Christian, the Bible teaches us that there will be no more suffering. Suffering is simply a fact of life. Everyone will suffer at some point and time in some area or another. We will experience suffering, whether it be mental, emotional, physical, or spiritual. The Bible states, "Man that is born of a woman is of few days and full of trouble" (Job 14:1). For this reason, no one is immune to suffering. Jesus states in, "In the world ye shall have tribulation" (Jn. 16:33). Paul further states, "Yea, and all that will live godly in Christ Jesus shall suffer persecution" (2 Tim. 3:12). Paul again writes in Romans 8:17, "And if children, then heirs; heirs of God, and joint-heirs with Christ; if so be that we suffer with him, that we may be also glorified together." The Apostle Peter puts suffering in a practical sense when he writes in 1 Peter 2:21, "For even hereunto were ye called: because Christ also suffered for us, leaving us an example, that ye should follow his steps."Suffering Ends Suffering ceases to exist for a child of God when they die. Revelation 21:4 states that in heaven "neither shall there be any more pain." For those who put their faith and trust in Jesus Christ for salvation, physical death is the end of all suffering forever and ever. But for those who refuse Christ, their suffering has only begun. In Mark 16:25, Jesus relates a tale of two individuals. One was a rich man who seemed to live in the lap of luxury. The other man was Lazarus, a homeless beggar who also suffered from physical problems. Jesus states that both eventually died.

However, the rich man, who in this life suffered little, is now tormented in the flames of hell. Lazarus, in contrast to the rich man, is now comforted. We can know that in Christ, all suffering comes to an end with death.Sorrow Ends

We experience many sorrows in this life. We can experience sorrow during the time of sickness, or when someone dies or when tragic events occur in our life. Trouble is present at every turn.

But in John 14:1, Jesus states, "Let not your hearts be troubled." We can be at peace knowing that, in heaven, sorrow will be no more. We can be comforted in these times because we know He will never leave us nor forsake us. If we look at Revelation 21:4, we read that, in heaven, there will be "neither sorrow." Isaiah 35:10 states, "And the ransomed of the Lord shall return and come to Zion with songs and everlasting joy upon their heads: they shall obtain joy and gladness, and sorrow and sighing shall flee away." Isaiah 65:19 tells us that God will joy in His people in heaven and that there will not be any further weeping or crying. Praise God that in heaven we will never again feel sorrowful for any reason.Sickness Ends

At some point in our lives, we have all experienced sickness. Sickness can take many forms whether it's a common cold, the flu, or even something more serious like heart disease or cancer, sickness occurs in the life of every individual. Due to the curse of sin, these fleshly bodies over time begin to wear down and finally wear out. The Bible states that it is once appointed unto man to die. The ratio of death to individuals is 1:1. All will die. God, in His word, gives us another comforting thought. In Revelation 21:4, the Bible states, "There shall be no more death." Death is forever wiped away in heaven. The Apostle Paul writes in 1 Corinthians 15:54–57, "So when this corruptible shall have put on incorruption, and this mortal shall have put on immortality, then shall be brought to pass the saying that is written, Death is swallowed up in victory. O death, where is thy sting? O grave, where is thy victory? The sting of death is sin; and the strength of sin is the law. But thanks be to God, which giveth us the victory through our Lord Jesus Christ." Death is no longer is victorious. It no longer has any sting. Death entirely has been swallowed up. For God so loved the world, that he gave his only begotten Son, that whosoever believeth in him should not perish, but have everlasting life." In heaven, there will never be another sickness or another death. We are victorious over death through Jesus Christ our Lord.Separation Ends.

The Bible states that when we are absent from the body, we are present with the Lord. It is wonderful and comforting to know that as children of God, the moment that we close our eyes in death, we are instantaneously transported into the presence of God. We see that to be true in looking back at Lazarus. In Luke 16:22, we read that Lazarus, upon dying, was carried by the angels into Abraham's bosom. In John 14:3, Jesus gives us the reason why our hearts should not be troubled. He states, "And if I go and prepare a place for you, I will come again, and receive you unto myself; that where I am, there ye may be also." I find it interesting that in writing of the new heaven and earth in Revelation, John states there is no more sea.Surely, we can see that literally there will be no great body of water there, but I believe that John was relating something from his heart by mentioning it. John has been exiled by the Roman government to the Isle of Patmos. This island was simply a Roman penal colony off the coast of Asia Minor, and it was separated from the mainland by the Aegean Sea. I believe

John equated the absence of the sea to be the absence of that barrier which separated him from all those whom he loved. When we look at the description of the new heaven and earth, we see an absence of anything that would hinder us from complete fellowship with Christ. What a glorious thing it will be when we see Christ face to face and are united with loved ones who have gone. The death of a Christian is precious because it releases them from the suffering, the sickness, and the separation and pain of this life. We must align our perspective on death with God's perspective. God has an eternal perspective that we sometimes can't seem to grasp. We are saddened with the loss of a loved one, but it brings joy to God's heart when a believer passes from this life to be in His presence.

We must not charge God foolishly when a loved one is taken from us, but learn to appreciate the time that we had with them when they were with us. As the saying goes, "Two things in life are sure- death and taxes," but the two things that are absolutely sure are death and judgment. Will you be prepared?Paul, at the end of his life, wrote these words in 2 Timothy 4:6–8, "For I am already being poured out like a drink offering, and the time has come for my departure. I have fought the good fight, I have finished the race, and I have kept the faith. Now there is in store for me the crown of righteousness, which the Lord, the righteous Judge, will award to me on that day—and not only to me, but also to all who have longed for his appearing." Many times, life seems more like a fight than anything else. We get knocked down, and God helps us back up. We face health concerns that seem like an uphill battle, but we go on. We come to a time like this and we face grief and we need help from God to continue. I encourage you to never give up. Ecclesiastes 9:11 says, "The race is not given to the swift, nor the battle to the strong, but to the one who will endure to the end."I felt many times like quitting and giving up, but something inside of me just would not let me throw in the towel. I know it was the Holy Spirit pushing me to stay in the race. I had wept, and I knew my joy was coming in the morning.

Chapter 4

Viewing Life and the Transition of Death from an Eternal Perspective

Most of us have experienced the loss of a loved one. If we have not, it is more than likely that at some point we will. All of the passages of scripture that I've been sharing with you will hopefully help you look at death from a different perspective. It is imperative that we get a proper biblical understanding of death from God's perspective. This will not only help us, but we will also be able to help others as well. Correct information leads to right thinking. Transition will come to your family. It does not matter how anointed you are, it does not matter about how beautiful you are, or how much money you make, your skin color, even your job doesn't matter. Death does not have favorites. Ultimately, the only thing that matters is the fact that we have a relationship with God and only what we do for Christ will last. The word of God will bring the assurance that we need to get us through. Here are some additional scriptures that you might consider. For my Father's will is that everyone who looks to the Son and believes in him shall have eternal life, and I will raise him up at the last day. (Jn. 6:40) Life is precious and fragile, and James 4:14 tells us, "It is like a vapor." Hebrew 9:27 says, "We'll each die and then stand before God." Science states that one hundred percent of all humans will die. Just like birth is the passage from the womb to life on earth, death is the passage between this life and eternity. As a believer, your life and death are in God's hands. All the days ordained for me were written in your book before one of them came to be. (Ps. 139:16) Your death will be in God's perfect time according to His plan. Precious in the sight of the LORD is the death of his saints. (Ps. 116:15) Paul agreed saying to leave earth and be with Christ is better by far than life on this earth. (Phil. 1:23) Tells us that in an instant this earthly body will be replaced with a heavenly one. (1 Cor. 15:52)Unless a grain of wheat falls into the earth and dies, it remains alone; but if it dies, it bears much fruit. (Jn.12:24) Just like God has a purpose for your life, there will be a divine purpose in your death. And there's another interesting verse, which says, "The righteous are taken away to be spared from evil" (Isa. 57:1).We must come to grips with our own mortality, realizing that life is short, and this should motivate us to enjoy it and make the most of every day. Our mortality is something that we should take very seriously because one day, we will have to stand before the judgment seat of Christ. We must be aware of the fact that we will have to spend eternity somewhere. Be very careful what you do in this life because it echoes through eternity. So we fix our eyes not on what is seen, but on what is unseen. For what is seen is temporary, but what is unseen is eternal. (2 Cor. 4:18)He has set eternity in our hearts. (Ecles. 3:11)We are in this world but not of it, we were made for eternity.We should be looking for our treasure in heaven?The kingdom of heaven is like treasure hidden in a field. When a man found it, he hid it again, and then in his joy went and sold all he had and bought that field. (Matt. 13:44)The only true hope we have is the hope we have in Christ.Jeremiah 29:11 and Ephesians 2:10 tell you, "God put you here for a specific purpose."1 Corinthians 3:10–15 tells us we are each building on the foundation of Christ using either gold, silver, and precious stones or wood hay and stubble. We are told the work of our life will be evaluated in eternity.

Chapter 5

Dealing With the Pain in General and Pressing Forward for Healing of the Soul

God does have a plan for our life. He formed us and knew us from our mother's womb. Woven into that plan is free choice and free will. It is God's desire that all men would come to Him and be saved. Even though He has a will for us, He has given us the ability to make a choice, and we may choose to align ourselves with God's plan or we may choose to reject it. God's plan for us is a good plan. We must keep in mind that when sin entered the world, it brought catastrophic events. We experience terrorism, murder, and many other types of calamities. Bad things do happen, but that's not God's will. God always has a plan set in motion. Just like when Joseph's brothers sold him into slavery, God used it to save the Jewish nation and ultimately to bring about the birth of the Savior. Joseph says in Genesis 50:20, "What men intended for evil, God used for good."What I hope that I am conveying to you is that God does have a good plan for your life, and God remains sovereign. What we need to do is align ourselves with the plan that God has for us. Often times, God will allow painful events to come into our lives that are really designed to be a blessing; but, sometimes, we cannot discern this immediately. We will eventually be able to look back and say like Joseph, "What men intended for evil, God will use for our good."All the events in the course of our normal lives often grip us with pain. I said before in a previous chapter that mine and my family's lives were gripped with the pain of a horrible and untimely death with our uncle. This kind of tragedy is hard to accept and believe as a part of God's perfect plan, when a careless driver takes the life of a loved one; but we have to accept the fact that bad things do happen to good people. God helped us to push past the pain, and be better people for it.If you read the story about king David in the Bible, you will find that this story is an excellent example of what I am talking about. God had a great plan for King David's life. The Prophet Samuel anointed him to be king over Israel. David chose to exercise his freewill and sinned with Bathsheba. He committed adultery with Bathsheba and had her husband, Uriah, killed. This sinful trail was certainly not part of God's plan for David. So God sent the Prophet Nathan to confront David (2 Sam. 12) and get him to see the other options for the plan. Nathan was used as part of God's "plan" to get David back on the plan. Repentance!

Forgiveness! They were all part of the plan. But there would be pain. The death of a child.David entered a period of mourning and fasting. He begged for God to spare the child. But on the seventh day, the baby died. And after the baby died, David got up, washed himself, changed his clothes, and went to the Tabernacle to worship; and afterwards, he ate. Even though David deviated from God's perfect plan for his life, he repented and was used greatly but God. So, friend, I'm also saying to you that God also has a plan for your life. We can see that even though David grieved after the death of his child, he did not let grief consume him. He continued to worship God the same we should even while grieving.We may experience heartache or pain for a season, but we must push past the pain and move back toward wholeness despite our anguish.

Unfortunately, this isn't what always happens. We often allow the pain of our past to continue to rule us in our present and to affect our future. Struggling to breathe in today's clean air while still choking on yesterday's toxins is not a good place to be, nor trying to drive in the present while looking through a rear-view mirror of the past.Heartache should only have a season; and when the season ends, we must get up and wash ourselves off and return to worship like David. We should not become devoted and enamored with grief. Grief should not become a chronic condition in our lives. At some point, God expects us to move on. David prayed that the life of the child would be spared, hoping to change the outcome. And when David realized that the outcome had been set in motion and could not be changed, he pushed past his pain toward healing and wholeness that included returning to worship and getting on with his life. We must do the same. Whenever my wife passed, I hurt. I was leading and bleeding at the same time.

Praising God with brokenness. Many days, I felt hopeless and that no one cared how I felt. But like David, I had to continue to worship God and remember His promises. Worshiping God with a broken heart is very painful, but I trusted Him. You cannot feel sorry for yourself because some things in life you have no control over. You must continue to trust God and get up from your pity party, and keep on marching. Life continues to go on, so you must keep on marching toward the Lord. Don't be hindered by the pain. I learned how to push past the pain. Every one of us has different levels of pain that God only knows that we can bear. It's not the same for everybody. Sometimes, confiding in a loyal and true friend may be the key to your survival. Sit down and talk with your pastor or pastors that can counsel you and help you deal with the pain. Find someone who can give you spiritual advice. You must get on with your life and keep pressing toward the goal that God has placed on your life. Get involved with a group of believers who have a vision to chase after God. Stay connected, stay involved in church, and become a part of a ministry within the church, it could be the men's ministry, women's ministry, or youth ministry, even getting back into the routine of your regular work week, whatever it is get connected. All these things can be helpful for your survival. Sometimes, the death of a loved one can drive a wedge in the family. The pain causes us sometimes to lash out at others. This is a time when you must not allow bitterness and animosity to enter in on top of the grief. This is a time for the family to pull together and support each other. We must never get into the blame game and talk about who was there and who didn't do anything for the deceased. Maybe there is someone who you might be holding a grudge against or have ill feelings toward, you must choose to make a decision to forgive that person who has hurt you. Unforgiveness will only hinder your healing process. If you fail to let go of the pain, the pain will continue to hold on to you. It is not worth holding on to. Let the Lord heal you of your brokenness, and with that, take away the grief. "Be confident to know that the Lord has a great plan for your life, and that his plans for you are not evil, but to give you a future and a hope" (Jer. 29:11).

Chapter 6

How to Overcome Loneliness after a Loved One Dies

Loneliness is one of the most miserable feelings a person can have. When you're lonely you may feel that nobody loves you. You may feel that nobody cares. Loneliness can make you feel that nobody even cares if you exist. But here is a fact: you don't have to be alone to feel lonely. You can feel lonely in a crowd. It's not the number of people around you that determines your loneliness. It's the relationship you have with them. One of the ways to overcome this feeling is to first and foremost remember that, as a Christian, we are never alone. The Lord has promised in His word that He will never leave us nor forsake us. We have already talked about surrounding yourself with a support system and interacting with others as a way of dealing with grief. We must continuously resist the desire to isolate ourselves. This might be the time to get out of your comfort zone and make yourself open to new experiences. You might even seek out opportunities to serve others in various capacities. And serving others can often times keep us from being too self -focused.After about one year and six months after the passing of my last spouse, loneliness began to set in. When you are accustomed to coming home to a wife and children, and no longer surrounded by the family being there, loneliness will eventually begin to take a toll on you. There were many days that I would come home and lie in bed thinking about my family. My family has always been my support. My children are all adults now with their own families. It is possible to overcome the grief of losing a loved one, but it will take some discipline and keeping your mind focused on the Lord. Coming home to an empty house can invoke a feeling of loneliness. You miss the laughter, the noise, and the playing of games with your wife and children; now, this is gone. Regardless of your station in life, you can still feel lonely. You can be wealthy, popular, or beautiful and still feel lonely. Everyone will experience loneliness at some point in their life. When familiar patterns are disrupted in our lives, this can bring feelings of loneliness. We have to remember that life is one transition after another, and many of these transitions can generate feelings of loneliness. Separation and isolation, being away from my spouse, were very hard to deal with. Knowing that I would never see her again in her physical body was a struggle. I had to face the reality that she was not coming back.

Regardless of the amount of tears I shed, her time in the earthly realm had expired. No matter how much you wish your loved one would come back, they are not. You must accept this reality as well. It was very difficult for me after coming home from work and seeing an empty house.

Walking into our shared closet I was flooded with memories. The whole closet was full of her aroma. All of her clothes still smelled like her. I was a very indulgent husband and loved showering her with gifts; because of this, not only was our closet filled with her things, but they were spread even to other bedroom closets in the house. She loved clothes, shoes, hats, purses, and perfumes. And they became a constant reminder that she was not here with me. I missed her so much that there were times I'd go through her things in the closet just to smell her scent. I never would have thought that having her clothing around the house would cause memories to flood me, and with those memories came back the grief of having lost her. It was difficult for me to make up my mind to donate her things and press forward. It took me a year and a half to make the decision. To those of you that have suffered loss, this may be something that can help you heal. Keeping some items to remember your loved one would certainly be reasonable, but most things would be served well to be donated or gifted to someone else. This has helped me tremendously. I was able to gift her things and be a blessing to someone in need. I missed her so much that whenever I went to bed, I found myself grabbing hold of her pillows and embracing them thinking it was her. Sometimes, it's not the big things to release in life to move forward, it's the little things that keep us from complete healing. I know that my wife would have wanted me to move on with my life. Let the Lord heal you of your brokenness and know that there is life after death, for not only your loved one in Christ, but for you as well.I'd like to share a dream with you that I had after the death of my third wife, Dede. About two weeks after I buried her, she came to me in a dream. In the dream, the telephone rang, and I picked it up. I said, "Hello?" and she said, "Hey, honey, how are you doing?" I asked her, "When was she coming home?" She said to me, "That she could not come home but that I would see her again." In the dream, she began thanking me for giving her such a good life and for being such a good husband. I kept telling her that I missed her very much and asked her to come home as soon as she could. There was silence for a moment, and she said to me, "This is not goodbye, I will see you later. I love you." I woke up from this dream with a feeling of sadness and loneliness.About a year and three months after her passing, I had another dream in which she told me to let her go. I told her that I could not let her go because she was my wife, and I loved her very much. In the dream, she repeatedly asked me to release her, but I continued to tell her that I couldn't let her go. An amazing thing happened in the dream; my mother-in-law walked in the room and told me to listen to Dede. She said, "You must let my daughter go if you're going to move on with the plans that God has for your life." I can remember in the dream weeping all over again. With great hesitation and sadness I said to Mother Stacey (my mother-in-law), "I will." When I said this, I could feel the Lord giving me a sense of peace in the dream. When I woke up, I immediately knew what God was saying to me. I had to release her, let her go, and begin to move forward with my life.I had good days, and I had bad days; and I know that's normal. I've always enjoyed my work as a pastor and as a businessman, and I've always been diligent in fulfilling my responsibilities. But when my wife died, to keep from becoming depressed and sad, I became a total workaholic, not taking time to eat properly and rest. Keeping busy can be therapeutic; but when you neglect other areas of your life, not getting enough rest and not eating properly, working yourself to exhaustion can take a toll on you physically, mentally, and spiritually. The other problem that accrues from this is that I had to realize that I had children and other family members that needed my love and support. Try not to allow yourself to fall into the pattern of staying constantly busy. Others in an attempt to deal with the grief become shopaholics trying to fill the void with material things, not knowing that the happiness they get from these things will only last temporarily. Some even turn to drugs and alcohol, or even try to escape through a fantasy world of books, TV, or games. Other people may just do nothing—literally nothing—but hold a never-ending pity party. Some people attempt to isolate themselves from others, not knowing that this can be devastating to the healing process because as I stated before, you need the support of others. I, myself, may have of been guilty of this, but we need love and interaction from the people we love. We must also be careful to not isolate God. If we can recognize God's presence is with us, we can survive anything. Where is God when you're lonely? He is right there. There is no place where God is not. He is everywhere at every time, and you can constantly talk with Him. Don't forget that prayer is a fantastic tool that you can continue to use during these times. Talk to God, and let Him speak to you. We must continue to rely on God's strength to make it through. God is stronger than your loneliness. I cannot emphasize too much how that serving others can help us with the healing process. It takes our mind off of ourselves and allows us to use the fuel of grief to help others. Do all the good you can. By all the means you can. In all the ways you can. In all the places you can. At all the times you can. To all the people you can. As long as ever you can.—John Wesley There is a joy that comes from serving and helping others.

Chapter 7

After the Grieving Process, We Must Hold On to the Promises of God

Never in my wildest dreams would I have ever imagined that I would lose three wives over a span of a few years. I believe that the Lord allowed me to experience all of these trials and tribulations so that I could share my testimony of how God can keep you no matter how severe the trials you may suffer. I am convinced that in spite of what has transpired in my life, that God loves me. I had a lot of questions running through my mind. Why God? Why me? I went through a period of time in my life where I thought God was intentionally punishing me for some type of wrong doing. At one point in my life, I had even become angry with God because of the great losses. I knew that my life was pleasing to God, I also knew that I hadn't done anything wrong, similar to Job in the Bible. I had to accept the fact that God was working out His sovereign will in my life even though I confess that I don't understand it all. I had to repent to God for thinking this way, and I know the Lord has forgiven me and has given me peace. I trust God. Destiny and purpose have to be fulfilled in your life if you are a believer in Christ. I am still learning that being a Christian is not always easy. The Bible is clear that suffering is a part of the Christian life. The Bible says, "If we suffer with Him, we shall also reign with Him" (2 Tim. 2:12). At this point, I'm going to share with you some additional things that I had to deal with as it relates to the death of my spouses and other family members. Saying goodbye is very hard. Grief hurts, but God's promises will bring us through! Everyone has endured or will endure the loss of a loved one at some time or another. All losses to a certain extent can bring an element of sadness into our lives whether the loss occurred five months ago or five years ago. Losing a precious loved one is not something that you "get over," but it will take time to heal from the experience of loss.One has to be careful that depression does not become a chronic condition in your life. Even though depression can be a normal reaction to loss, the enemy can use depression as a means of destroying you. Taking care to follow some of the suggestions I've given you can become the weapon you need to defeat depression. I found myself fighting against depression with the loss of each of my spouses. It was like going around the same old mountain. I felt like this was never going to end. But I can tell you now that I am victorious! I can also say that I am closer to God.Sometimes, it may seem as if we encounter the same trials multiple times, but remember that with each test, God will give you a testimony, which will enable us to bless others.

Experience is a great teacher if you learn the lesson from the experience. I believe that I had to go through these things to be able to help others who might be dealing with similar things.Here are a few more things I learned during my process of grief that I'd like to share with you. Grief is the silent, knife-like terror, and sadness that comes a hundred times a day when you catch yourself starting to speak to someone who is no longer there. Grief is the helpless wishing that things were different when you know they are not and never will be again. Grief is a whole cluster of adjustments, apprehensions, and uncertainties that strike life in its forward progress and make it difficult to redirect the energies of life. Grief is the emptiness that comes when you eat alone after eating with another for many years. I would have my meals and feel alone because my wife was no longer around to eat with me.I felt bad that I no longer had my wife to laugh with after eating supper. When my workday was over, all I wanted to do was go home and go to bed. I had no desire to be around anyone. Not only was my heart broken from my wife passing, but it was like somebody just took my heart right out of my body and cut it into pieces. I felt completely broken.I would get up to go to work; and, again, I felt like a dead man walking among the living. Feelings of emptiness and sadness took hold of me. There were even times that I felt like something was wrong with me. The enemy wanted me to feel like I was the cause of my wife's death. Whenever you are accustomed to being with someone you love for a long period of time and they are no longer there, it feels awkward. It feels as though you are out of place. All of this seemed very strange to me. I had to adjust myself to a new routine. Not being able to say good night to my wife, embrace, talk to her, or put my arms around her was very painful for me. How do I find a new normal? Things cannot go back to the way they were, so you must continue to move forward in your life. It can become very difficult at times, but you can do it with the help of the lord.For a while, I just didn't want to talk about this subject at all. I did not want to accept the reality that my wife was gone. But I've learned that it does help to confide in someone that you can trust and open up to. This is a part of the healing process. God sent friends into my life. Other pastors and fellow believers encouraged me, and these relationships were invaluable to me. The Lord orchestrated that they would call me at the exact times that I needed encouragement.Nothing that happens to us comes as a surprise to God.

Things might come as a shock and surprise to us, but God in His infinite wisdom orchestrates the events of our lives. Grief will come in our lives. No one is immune to it. But for the child of God, we are not without hope! The Bible tells us in Romans 8:28, "And we know that all things work together for good to them that love God, to them who are called according to His purpose." Remember these words of Jesus in John 14:1, "Let not your heart be troubled: ye believe in God, believe also in me." We can also be encouraged by the fact, as we have fore-stated, that our loved ones who have died in the Lord are in His presence now. Paul states in Philippians 1:21, "For to me to live in Christ, and to die is gain."Though we know these verses and even believe them, sometimes, we may be blinded or consumed by our grief. It is always good to go to the word of God as our resource for comfort. God has given us promises that will help us in our moments of sorrow. Psalms 121:1–2 tells us, "I will look to the hill from whence cometh my help, because my help comes from the Lord." I admonish you to trust the Lord even when you don't understand the whys, ifs, ands, or buts. Trust him in your grief, trust him in your pain, trust him in your loss, trust him in your setbacks, and trust him even when you don't feel like it.

Psalms 34:19 says, "Many are the afflictions of the righteous but

God will soon deliver you from them all."We don't have all the answers concerning what happens to the believer when they draw their last breath. But we can be assured of this one thing, that our loved ones who have died in the Lord are resting in the presence of God. These are all the promises of God that we can lean on to carry us through the grieving process. I had to read the word constantly, it helped me to keep pushing and not give into the pain. God will speak to you and comfort and encourage you through His word. I had to realize that I was a human being and that I was not exempt from suffering.Many times, when our loved ones pass away, it is after a long-term illness. We have to endure the difficulty of watching them suffer and fight for their life. I've experienced this first hand multiple times. I watched my wife suffer with cancer and have to endure the rigorous routine of being treated with chemotherapy. There were times she was so weak from treatments that the simple act of standing was near impossible. Seeing my best friend go through the multiple treatments, tests, and scans were very difficult. But I'm so grateful that God gave me the grace to be able to stand and be with her in the midst of it all.One day, Jesus will return for His people. Those who are alive will be "caught up" and taken to heaven with Him. When He comes, we will leave the troubles of this world behind. "And there shall in no wise enter into it anything that defileth, neither whatsoever worketh abomination, or maketh a lie: but they which are written in the Lamb's book of life" (Rev. 21:27). And this "grief" that we speak of will not follow us home! Saved friend, we have a promise of rest. We have seen Jesus through the eyes of faith, but one day, we will see Him face to face! "Beloved, now are we the sons of God, and it doth not yet appear what we shall be: but we know that, when he shall appear, we shall be like him; for we shall see him as he is" (1 Jn. 3:2). Jesus said in John 14:3, "I will come again, and receive you unto myself; that where I am, there ye may be also." We will spend eternity with our Savior who redeemed us!And God shall wipe away all tears from their eyes; and there shall be no more death, neither sorrow, nor crying, neither shall there be any more pain: for the former things are passed away. (Rev. 21:4)In this world, there is sickness, pain, death, sorrow, grief, and crying. But for those who know Jesus, we have hope! Grief will come. It is hard to say goodbye, but God's promises will help us make it through! The only way to have access to these promises is to have a personal relationship with Jesus Christ. God has devised a plan whereby sinners, who are his enemies, can be reconciled to Him and go to heaven when they die. Some of you who are reading this book and do not know Christ, I want you to know that you can give your life to Christ today and make a reservation to be reunited with your loved ones.I pray that my living testimony will be able to help you in some form or another so that you can get on with your life. I thank God for my children, all of my grandchildren, my church family, and all my friends who have poured into me. It is a fact that we need each other and that we are our brother's keeper.To the one who has read this book, I pray that you align your life with the will that God has for you. God is love, He is patient, caring, long suffering, giving, merciful, understanding, and He is a healer and restorer of the soul. Friend, God loves you and wants to have a relationship with you.Death is not the end, it is the beginning of new life to those who are born again. Let us ask the Lord to help us grieve as those with hope, not as those who are hopeless and to help us walk in His strength and power.Father, I pray that you would comfort the hearts of those that have lost loved ones.

Embrace them in your love and give them the assurance that you will never leave them nor forsake them. Restore every broken heart in Jesus name. May the Lord keep you and order your steps.Bishop John Chris Brown

About the Author

Bishop John Chris Brown, is a native of Amarillo, Texas, where for the past ten years, he has pastored a growing community church. He is the father of four children and six grandchildren, and he is the founder and CEO of Brown Insurance Agency. Bishop Brown is an active member of the community, and his commitment to the body of Christ is unparalleled. It is not uncommon for him to visit and pray for the sick and afflicted throughout the Amarillo area. As a sower sows seeds in the natural, Bishop Brown also sows seed unto God through ministry. He has experienced immeasurable loss in his lifetime, but has demonstrated unwavering faith and has devoted his life and service to the ministry. It is his strong faith and relationship with God that has seen him through the loss of three wives, his mother, spiritual father and mother, and his uncle all in the span of a few years. He has been called a modern-day Job. He has remained faithful in trusting God and engaging in kingdom work. He is one who has mentored, advised, and prayed others through their loss. Bishop Brown's ultimate desire is to see the people of God fully embrace God's love and walk in victory as they experience the fullness of God's promises.

www.ingramcontent.com/pod-product-compliance
Lightning Source LLC
Chambersburg PA
CBHW051250120626
46547CB00014B/1882